Learning Mathematics with the Abacus

Year 1

by
Sheikh Faisal Sheikh Mansor
Jamaluddin bin Sabran

KREATIF KEMBARA

KREATIF KEMBARA SDN. BHD.

ISBN : 983-9278-31-2
© KREATIF KEMBARA SDN. BHD.

KREATIF KEMBARA SDN. BHD.
11, 1st floor, Jalan Mewah, SS22/11, Damansara Jaya, 47400 Petaling Jaya, Selangor.
Tel : 03-77284400 / 77269431
Fax : 03-77284434
Email : admin@kreatifkembara.com
Printed by : Swan Printing Sdn. Bhd.

Contents

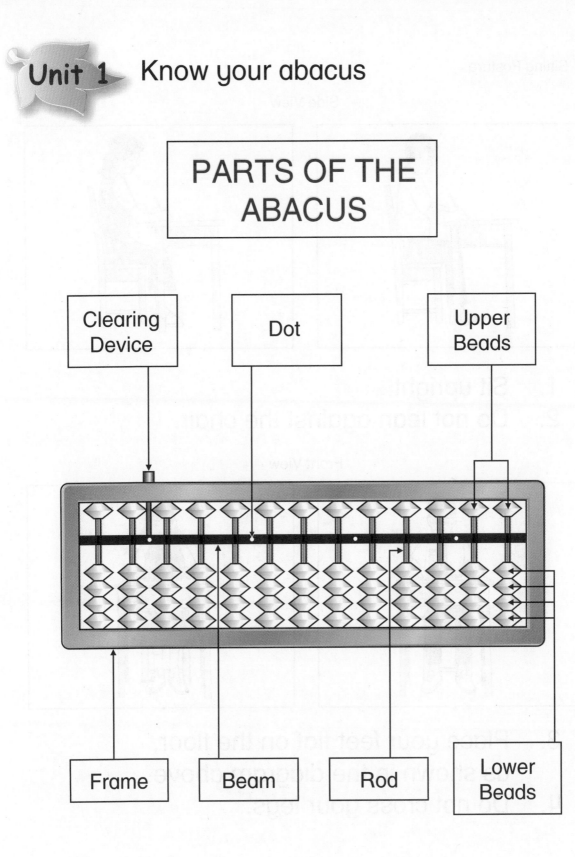

PARTS OF THE ABACUS

Clearing Device

Dot

Upper Beads

Frame

Beam

Rod

Lower Beads

Side View

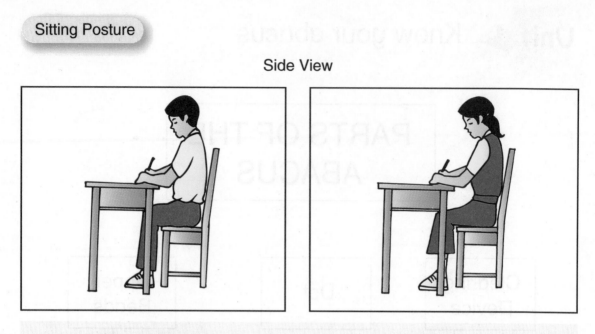

1. Sit upright.
2. Do not lean against the chair.

Front View

3. Place your feet flat on the floor, as shown in the diagram above.
4. Do not cross your legs.

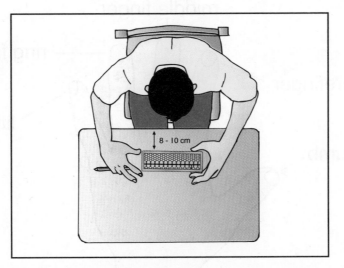

6. Place the middle finger of your left hand on the clearing device.
7. Your arms must not touch the table.
8. Place the abacus about 10 centimetres away from the edge of the table.

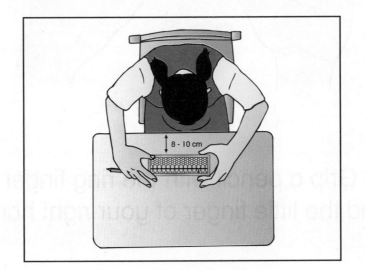

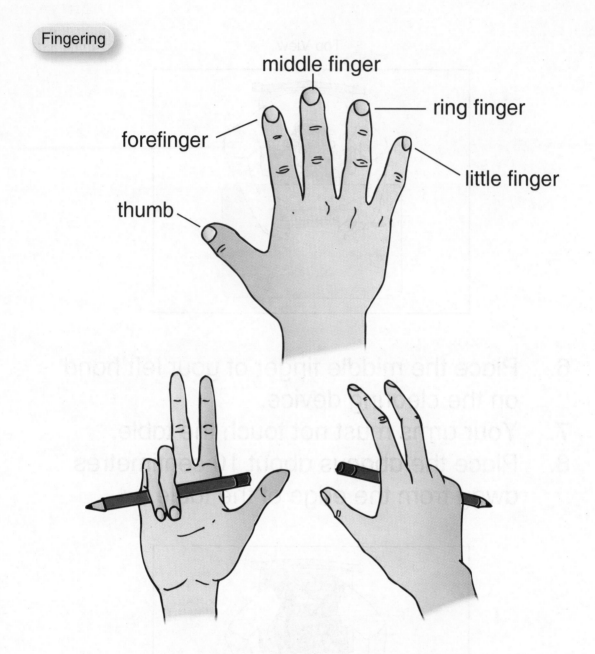

middle finger

ring finger

forefinger

little finger

thumb

Grip a pencil with the ring finger
and the little finger of your right hand.

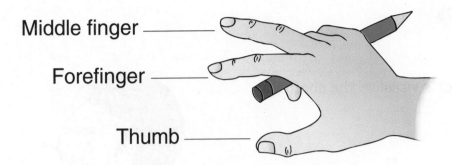

Middle finger

Forefinger

Thumb

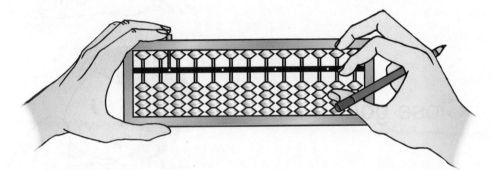

THUMB
The thumb moves the lower beads towards the beam.
(move up lower beads)

FOREFINGER
The forefinger moves the lower beads away from the beam.
(move down lower beads)

MIDDLE FINGER
The middle finger moves the upper beads towards
and away from the beam.
(move up and move down upper beads)

Visualising

Let's visualise the abacus!

1. Lay down.

2. Close your eyes.

3. Visualise the frame, the beam, the rods, the upper beads and the lower beads.

Unit 2 Numbers 0 to 10

Let's say!

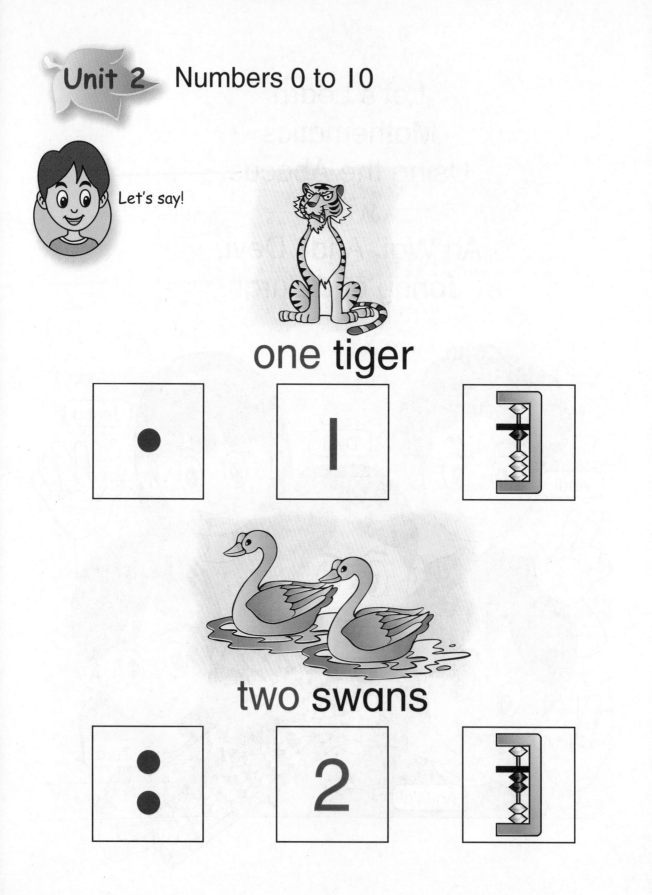

one tiger

• | (abacus)

two swans

: 2 (abacus)

three snakes

four flamingos

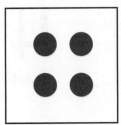

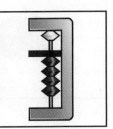

 Let's count!

Let's count the red apples.
How many red apples are there?

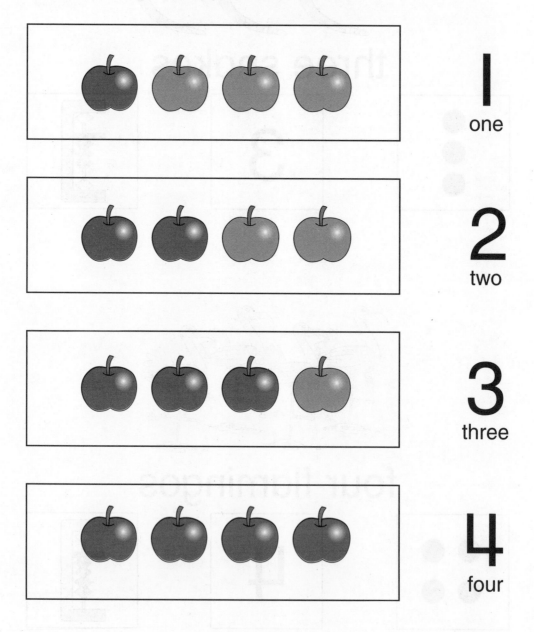

1 one

2 two

3 three

4 four

 Let's count with the beads!

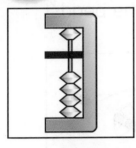 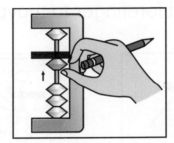 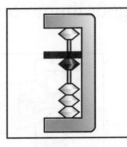 **I**
one

   **2**
two

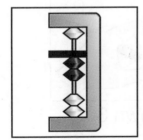  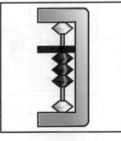 **3**
three

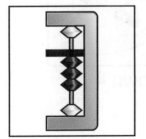  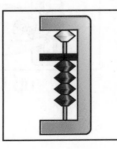 **4**
four

11

Use your thumb and forefinger to move the beads!

one

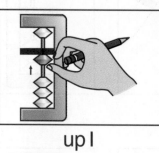
up 1

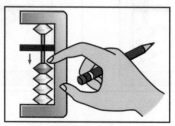
down 1

two

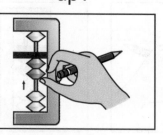
up 2

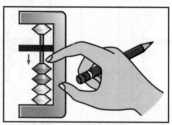
down 2

3
three

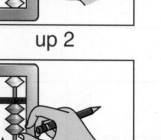
up 3

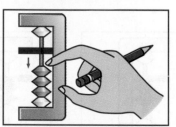
down 3

4
four

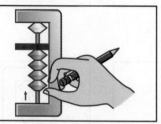
up 4

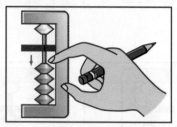
down 4

Let's write!

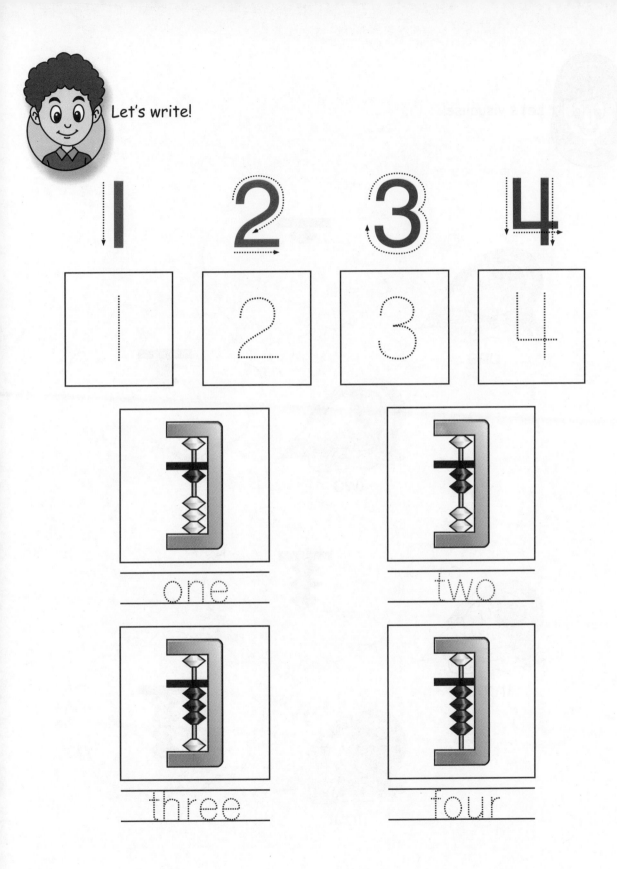

one

two

three

four

Let's visualise!

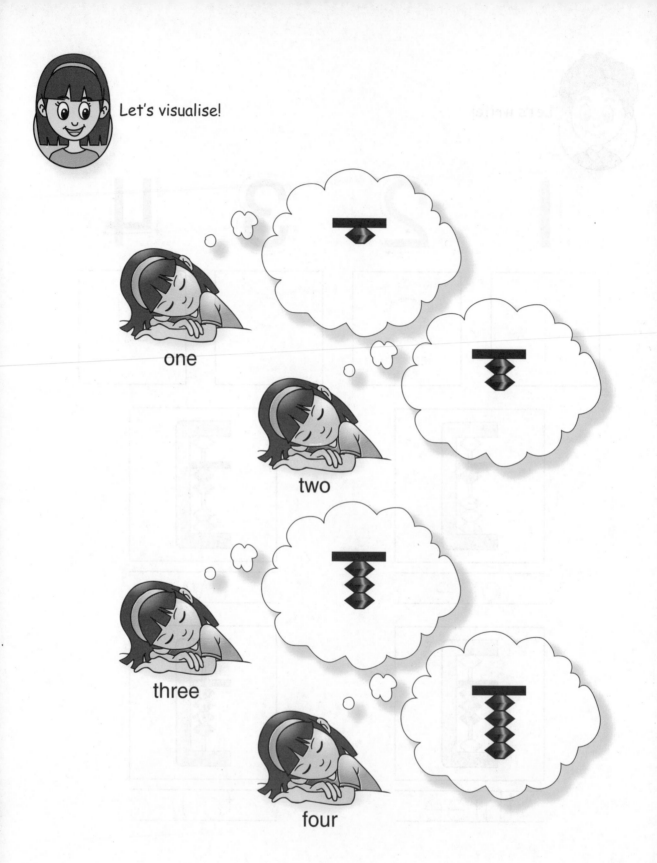

one

two

three

four

five rabbits

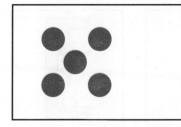  

six worms

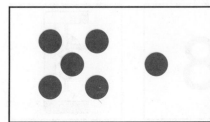  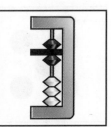

seven birds

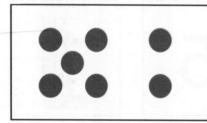  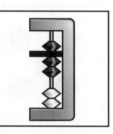

eight pandas

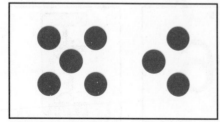  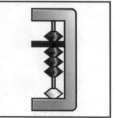

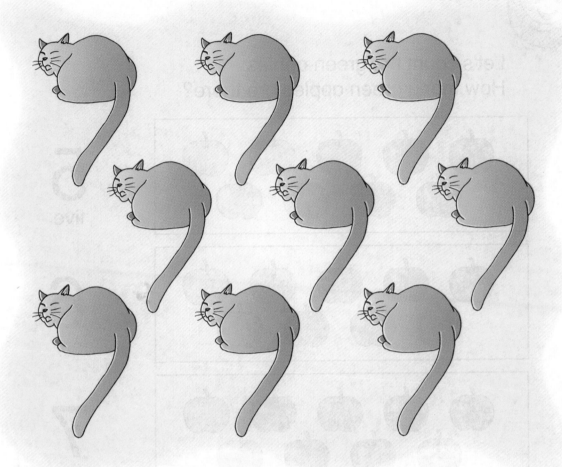

nine cats

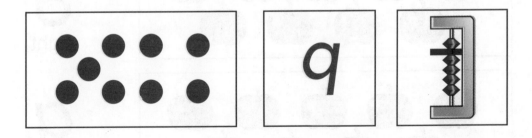

Let's count!

Let's count the green apples.
How many green apples are there?

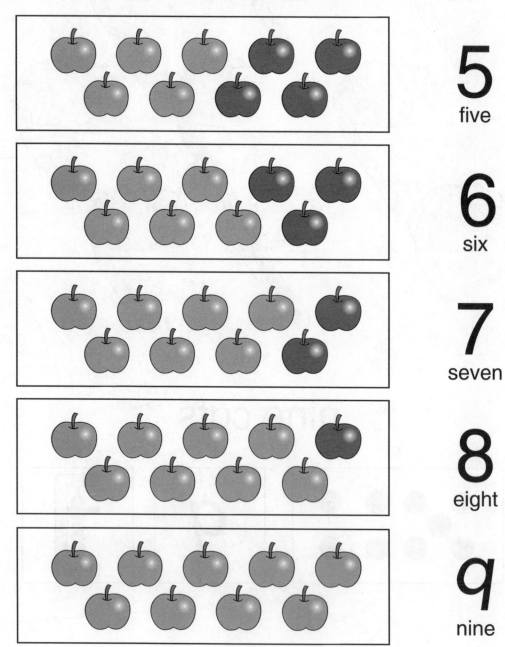

5 five

6 six

7 seven

8 eight

q nine

 Let's count with the beads!

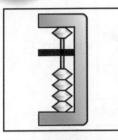 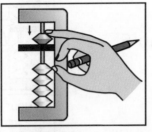 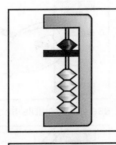 **5** five

 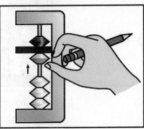  **6** six

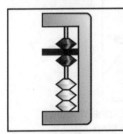 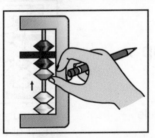 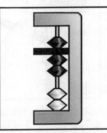 **7** seven

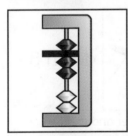   **8** eight

  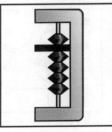 **q** nine

 Let's practise!

5 five

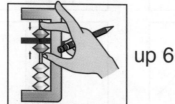 up 5

use your middle finger

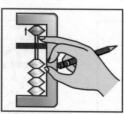 down 5

use your middle finger

6 six

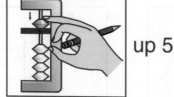 up 6

use your thumb and middle finger at the same time

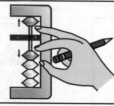 down 6

use your forefinger and middle finger at the same time

7 seven

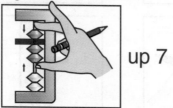 up 7

use your thumb and middle finger at the same time

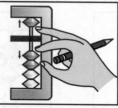 down 7

use your forefinger and middle finger at the same time

8 eight

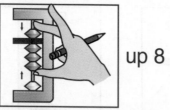 up 8

use your thumb and middle finger at the same time

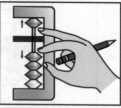 down 8

use your forefinger and middle finger at the same time

9 nine

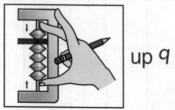 up 9

use your thumb and middle finger at the same time

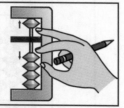 down 9

use your forefinger and middle finger at the same time

Let's write!

five   five

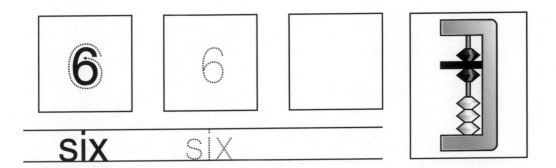

six   six

seven   seven

 Let's write!

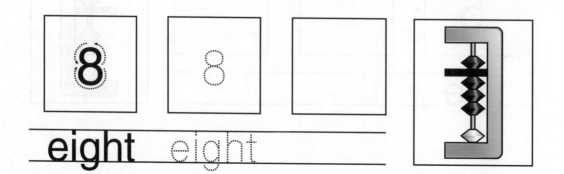

8   8

eight   eight

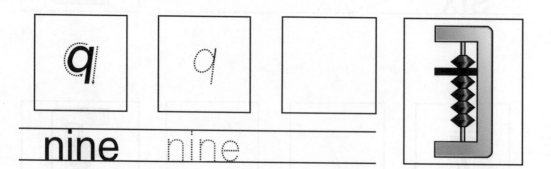

q   q

nine   nine

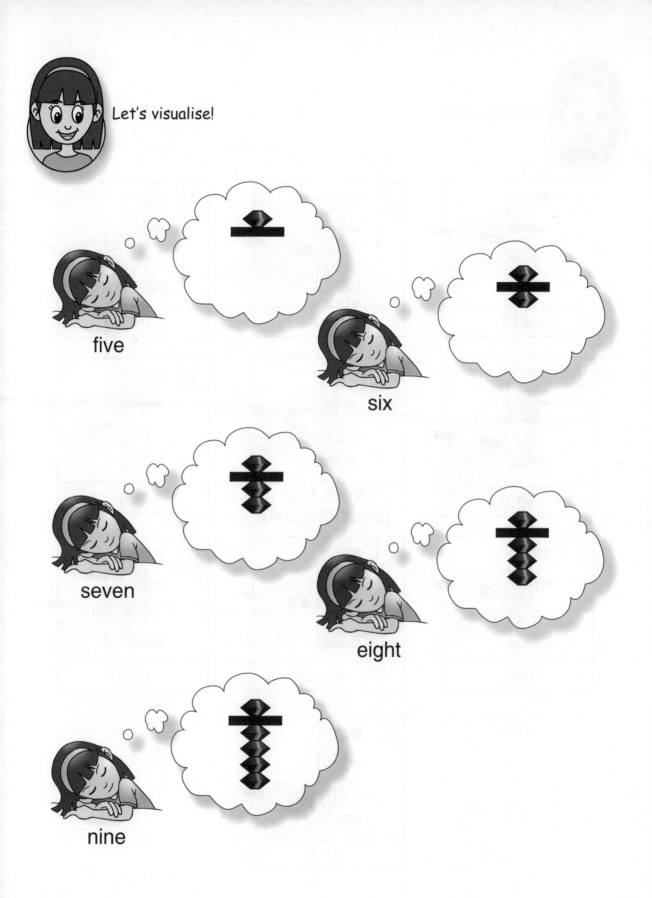

Let's visualise!

five

six

seven

eight

nine

Let's count on!

1	2	3
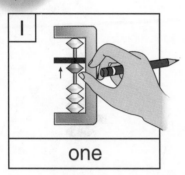	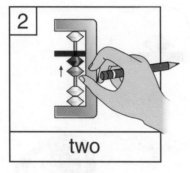	
one	two	three

4		5
	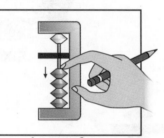	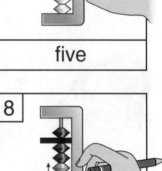
four	down four (clear abacus)	five

6	7	8
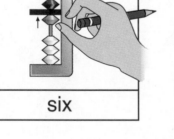	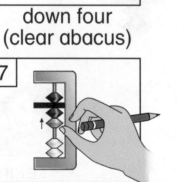	
six	seven	eight

q
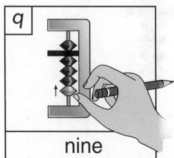
nine

 Let's count back!

9 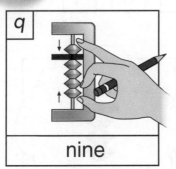 nine	**8** 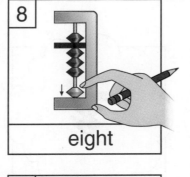 eight	**7** 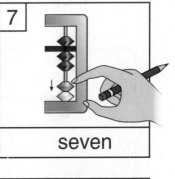 seven
6 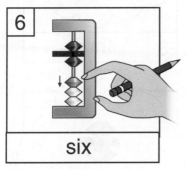 six	**5** 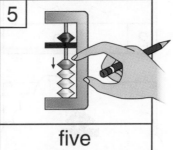 five	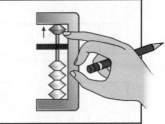 down five (clear abacus)
4 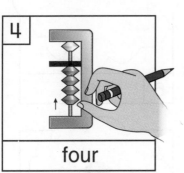 four	**3** 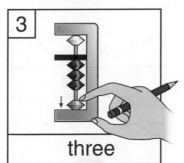 three	**2** 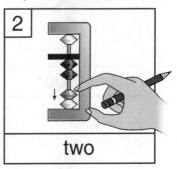 two
	1 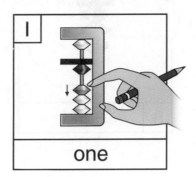 one	

| 1 | 2 | 3 | 4 | 5 | 6 | 7 | 8 | 9 |

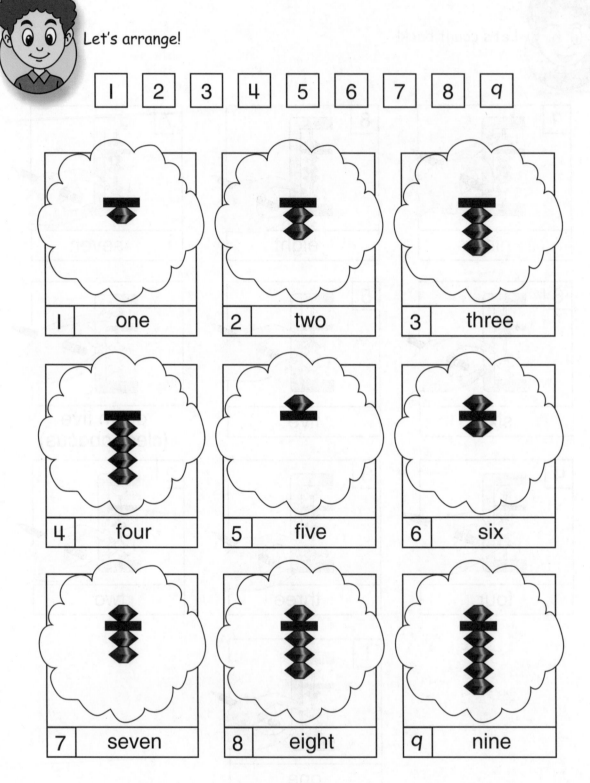

1	one	2	two	3	three
4	four	5	five	6	six
7	seven	8	eight	9	nine

Is there any carrot in the basket?

No.
There is none.
There is no carrot in the basket.
There is zero carrot.

zero

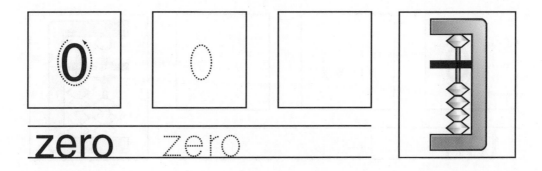

zero   zero

How many carrots are there in the basket now?
Let's count.

one, two, three, four,
five, six, seven, eight, nine, ten

There are ten carrots in the basket!

10

ten

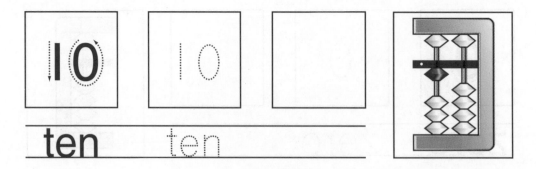

ten   ten

Let's read and write!

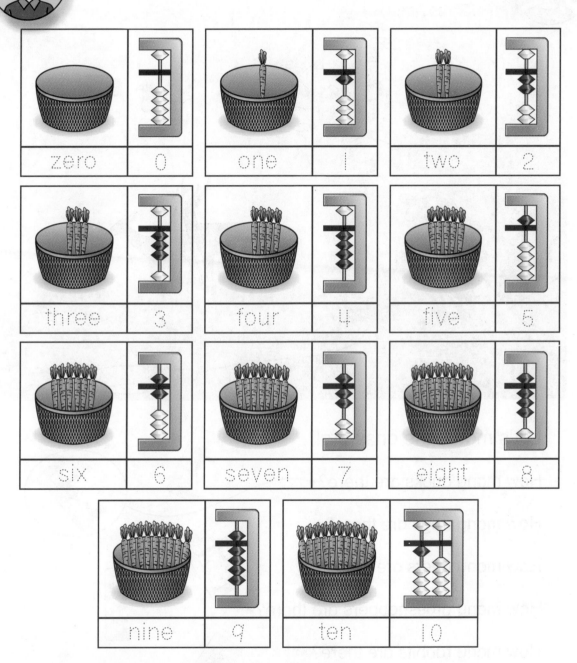

zero	0	one	1
two	2		
three	3	four	4
five	5		
six	6	seven	7
eight	8		
nine	9	ten	10

Can you write the missing numbers?

0	1		3		5			9	10

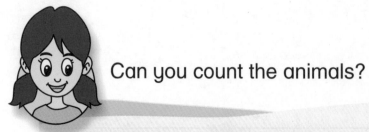

Can you count the animals?

Let's match the answers!

How many ducks are there? •

How many frogs are there? •

How many deers are there? •

How many grasshoppers are there? •

How many rabbits are there? •

How many bees are there? •

How many flamingos are there? •

How many parrots are there? •

How many tortoises are there? •

How many ants are there? •

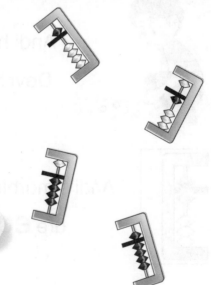

 Is there any tiger in the picture?

 Let's compare!

Ah Wai has **2** rabbits.

Zura has **2** rabbits too.

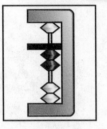

Ah Wai's and Zura's rabbits
are **equal** in number.

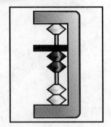

Andi has **6** marbles.

Devi has **6** flowers.

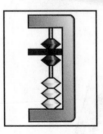

Andi's marbles and Devi's flowers
are **equal** in number.

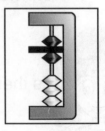

Zura has 5 balloons.
Jenny has 1 balloon.

Zura's and Jenny's balloons
are **not equal** in number.

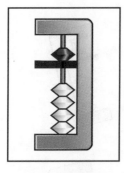

Zura has **more** balloons.
Jenny has **less** balloons.

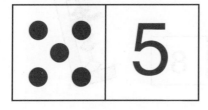

is **more** than
is **larger** than

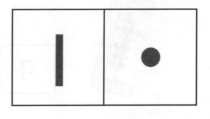

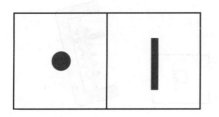

is **less** than
is **smaller** than

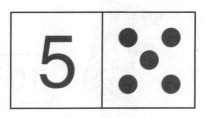

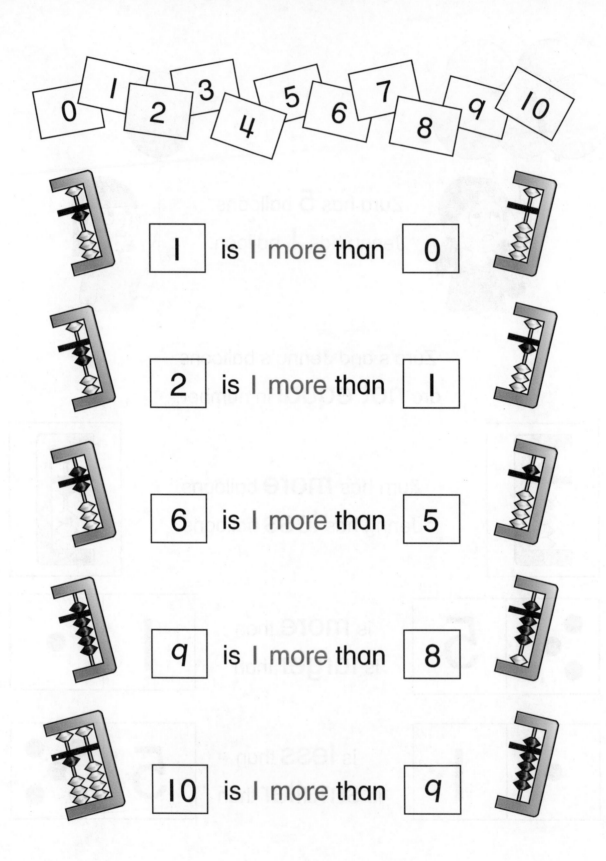

0 1 2 3 4 5 6 7 8 9 10

1 is 1 more than 0

2 is 1 more than 1

6 is 1 more than 5

9 is 1 more than 8

10 is 1 more than 9

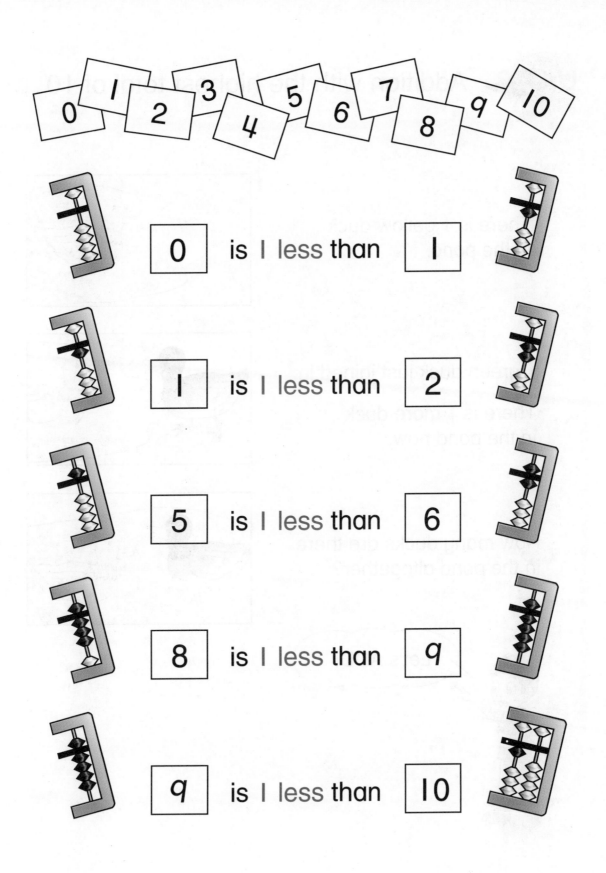

0 is 1 less than 1

1 is 1 less than 2

5 is 1 less than 6

8 is 1 less than 9

9 is 1 less than 10

There is 1 yellow duck
in the pond.

1 green duck just joined in.

There is 1 more duck
in the pond now.

How many ducks are there
in the pond altogether?

Let's ADD!

2 **is 1 more than** 1

1 and 1 more is 2

1 and 1 is 2
1 add 1 is 2
1 plus 1 is 2
1 plus 1 equals 2
1 + 1 = 2

How do we add using the abacus?

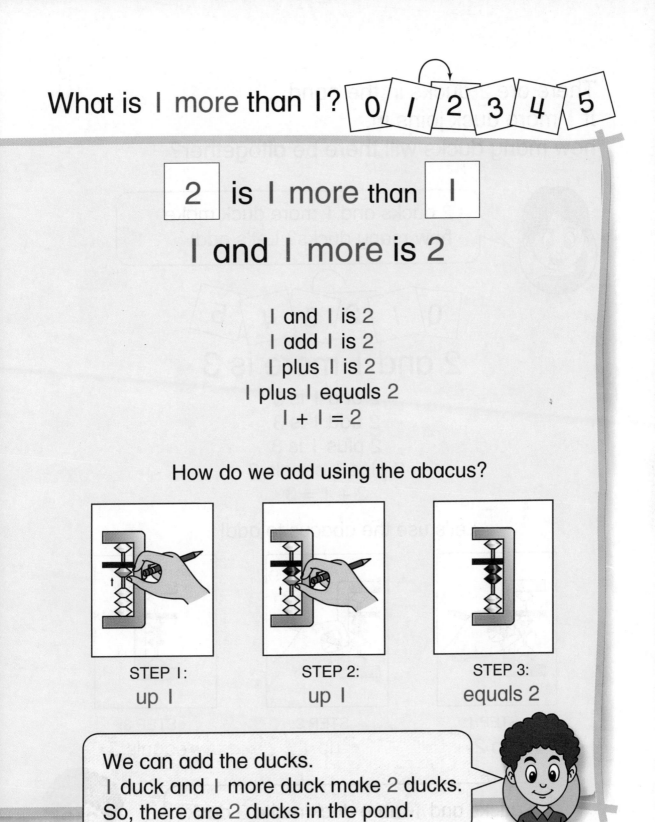

STEP 1:
up 1

STEP 2:
up 1

STEP 3:
equals 2

We can add the ducks.
1 duck and 1 more duck make 2 ducks.
So, there are 2 ducks in the pond.

There are 2 ducks in the pond.
If 1 more duck joins in,
how many ducks will there be altogether?

2 ducks and 1 more duck make
how many ducks? Let's add!

0 1 2 3 4 5

2 and 1 more is 3

2 and 1 is 3
2 add 1 is 3
2 plus 1 is 3
2 plus 1 equals 3
$2 + 1 = 3$

Let's use the abacus to add!

STEP 1:
up 2

STEP 2:
up 1

STEP 3:
equals 3

2 ducks and 1 more duck make 3 ducks.
There will be 3 ducks altogether.

Zura has 1 egg. Jenny has 2 eggs.

How many eggs are there altogether?
Let's add!

1 + 2 = ?

STEP 1:
up 1

STEP 2:
up 2

STEP 3:
equals 3

1 + 2 = 3

There are 3 eggs altogether!

Andi has 2 bags. Devi has 2 bags.

How many bags are there altogether?
Let's add!

$$2 \ + \ 2 \ = \ ?$$

STEP 1:
up 2

STEP 2:
up 2

STEP 3:
equals 4

$$2 \ + \ 2 \ = \ 4$$

There are 4 bags altogether!

Let's practise!

$1 + 1 = ?$

 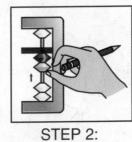 

STEP 1:
up 1

STEP 2:
up 1

STEP 3:
equals 2

$1 + 2 = ?$

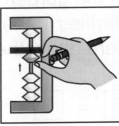 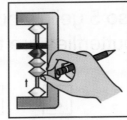 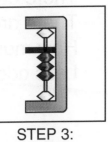

STEP 1:
up 1

STEP 2:
up 2

STEP 3:
equals 3

$3 + 1 = ?$

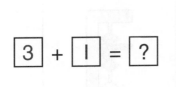

 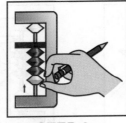 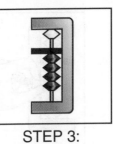

STEP 1:
up 3

STEP 2:
up 1

STEP 3:
equals 4

$2 + 2 = ?$

STEP 1:
up 2

STEP 2:
up 2

STEP 3:
equals 4

There are 2 red butterflies in the garden.
There are also 5 yellow butterflies in the garden.
How many butterflies are there altogether?
Let's add!

$$\boxed{2} + \boxed{5} = \boxed{?}$$

How do we add using the abacus?

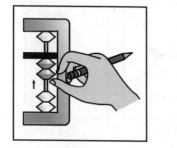

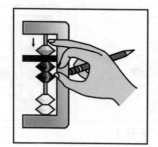

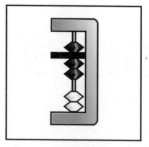

STEP 1:
up 2

STEP 2:
up 5

STEP 3:
equals 7

$$\boxed{2} + \boxed{5} = \boxed{7}$$

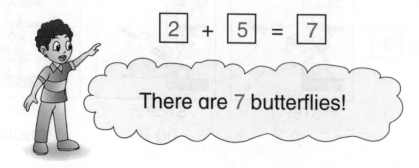

There are 7 butterflies!

Ah Wai has
6 rambutans.

Devi has
3 rambutans.

How many rambutans are there altogether?

 Let's add!

6 + 3 = ?

Let's use the abacus to add!

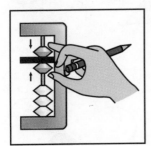

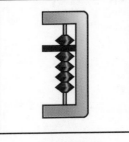

STEP 1:
up 6

STEP 2:
up 3

STEP 3:
equals 9

6 + 3 = 9

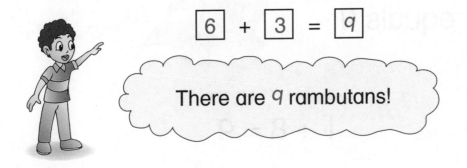

There are 9 rambutans!

 Let's visualise!

What is 1 + 8?

Step 1:   **1, up 1**

Step 2:   **plus 8, up 8**

Step 3:   **equals 9**

$$1 + 8 = 9$$

 Let's visualise!

What is 2 + 7?

Step 1: 2, up 2

Step 2: plus 7, up 7

Step 3: equals 9

2 + 7 = 9

 Let's count the apples!

How many apples are there altogether?
Let's count them!

There are 5 apples altogether.

How many apples are red?
Let's count!
There are 4 red apples!

How many apples are green?
Let's count again!
There is only 1 green apple!

4 red apples plus 1 green apple
equals 5 apples altogether!

$$4 + 1 = 5$$

 Let's count the bees!

How many bees are there altogether?
Let's count them!

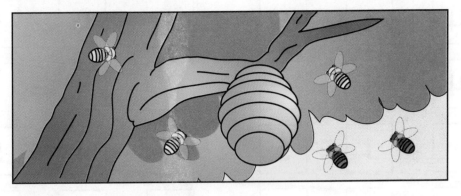

There are 5 bees altogether.

How many bees are yellow?
Let's count!
There are 3 yellow bees!
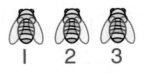

How many bees are brown?
Let's count again!
There are 2 brown bees!

3 yellow bees plus 2 brown bees
equals 5 bees altogether!

$$3 + 2 = 5$$

The Little Friend!

Let's write!

4	+	1	=	5
4	+	1	=	
	+	1	=	5
4	+		=	5

1	+	4	=	5
1	+	4	=	
	+	4	=	5
1	+		=	5

4 and 1 make 5

1 and 4 make 5

5
4   1

5
1   4

We say 1 is the Little Friend of 4

We say 4 is the Little Friend of 1

The Little Friend!

Let's write!

3	+	2	=	5
3	+	2	=	
	+	2	=	5
3	+		=	5

2	+	3	=	5
2	+	3	=	
	+	3	=	5
2	+		=	5

3 and 2 make 5

2 and 3 make 5

```
      5
     / \
    3   2
```

```
      5
     / \
    2   3
```

We say 2 is the Little Friend of 3

We say 3 is the Little Friend of 2

49

Let's add using the abacus!

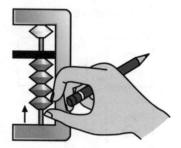

Step 1: 4, up 4

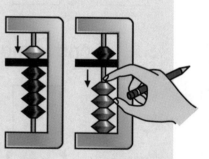

Step 2 : plus 1, up 1?

But there are not enough lower beads.

USE THE LITTLE FRIEND OF 1!

Think! What is the little friend of 1?
The little friend of 1 is 4.

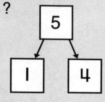

Up 5, Down little friend.

So, Up 5, Down 4

Step 3: equals 5

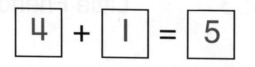

Let's add using the abacus!

$$3 + 2 = ?$$

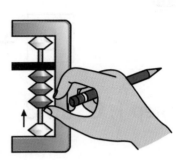

Step 1: **3, up 3**

Step 2 : plus 2, up 2?

But there are not enough lower beads.

USE THE LITTLE FRIEND OF 2!

Think! What is the little friend of 2?
The little friend of 2 is 3.

```
      5
     / \
    2   3
```

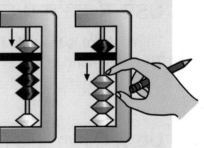

Up 5, Down little friend.

So, **Up 5, Down 3**

Step 3: **equals 5**

$$3 + 2 = 5$$

Let's practise!

$$3 + 3 = ?$$

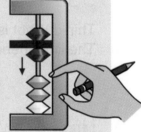

Step 1: 3, up 3

Step 2 : plus 3, up 3?

But there are not enough lower beads.

USE THE LITTLE FRIEND OF 3!

Think! What is the little friend of 3?
The little friend of 3 is 2.

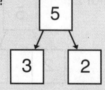

Up 5, Down little friend.

So, **Up 5, Down 2**

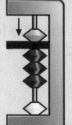

Step 3: equals 6

$$3 + 3 = 6$$

 Let's practise!

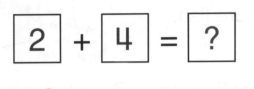

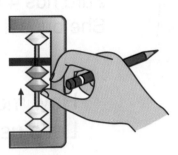

Step 1: 2, up 2

Step 2 : plus 4, up 4?

But there are not enough lower beads.

USE THE LITTLE FRIEND OF 4!

Think! What is the little friend of 4?
The little friend of 4 is 1.

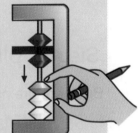

Up 5, Down little friend.

So, Up 5, Down 1

Step 3: equals 6

Let's add!

Zura has 4 fish.
She buys 4 more fish.

How many fish does Zura have now?
Let's use the abacus to calculate!

$$4 + 4 = ?$$

Step 1 : 4, up 4

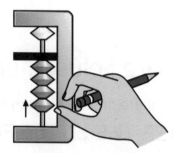

Step 2 : plus 4, up 4?

But there are not enough lower beads.

USE THE LITTLE FRIEND OF 4!

Think! What is the little friend of 4?
The little friend of 4 is 1.

Up 5, Down little friend.

So, Up 5, Down 1

5
4 1

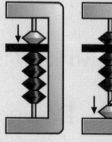

Step 3 : equals 8

$$4 + 4 = 8$$

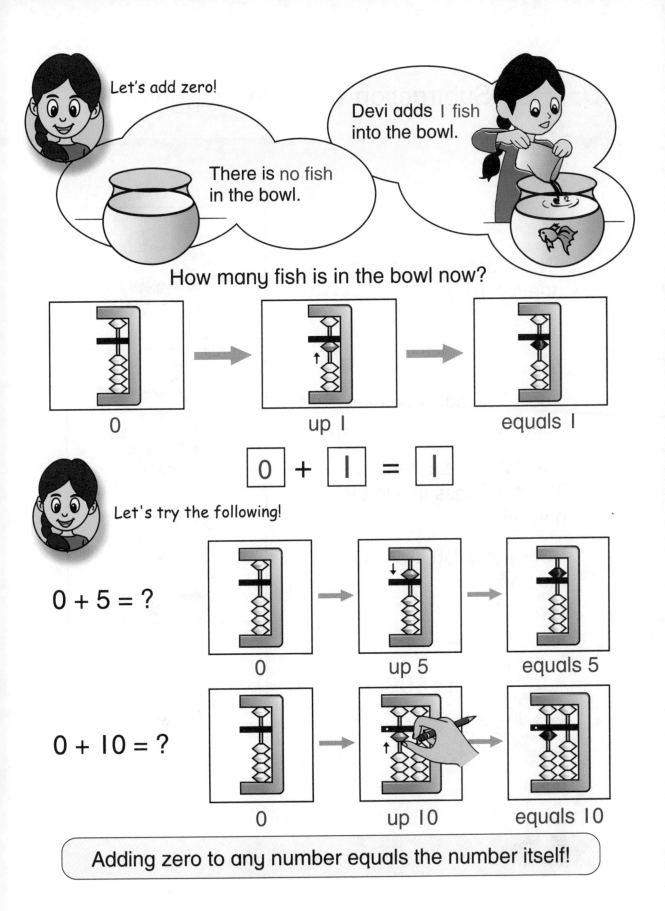

How many fish is in the bowl now?

0   up 1   equals 1

$$0 + 1 = 1$$

Let's try the following!

$0 + 5 = ?$

0   up 5   equals 5

$0 + 10 = ?$

0   up 10   equals 10

Adding zero to any number equals the number itself!

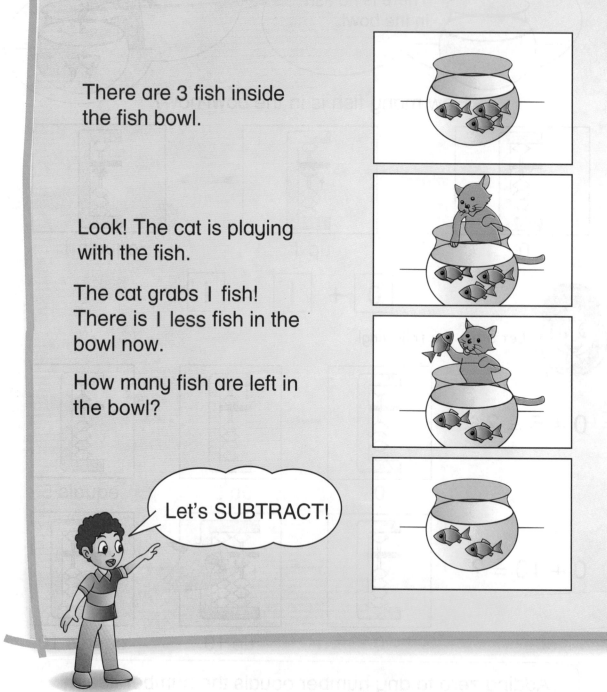

There are 3 fish inside the fish bowl.

Look! The cat is playing with the fish.

The cat grabs 1 fish! There is 1 less fish in the bowl now.

How many fish are left in the bowl?

Let's SUBTRACT!

What is I less than 3?

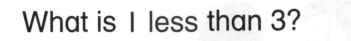

2 is I less than **3**

3 and I less is 2

3 subtract I is 2
3 take away I is 2
3 minus I is 2
3 minus I equals 2
3 − I = 2

How do we subtract using the abacus?

STEP I:
up 3

STEP 2:
down I

STEP 3:
equals 2

We can subtract the fish.
3 fish minus I fish is 2 fish.
So, there are 2 fish left in the bowl.

Zura has 4 eggs. Zura gives Jenny 1 egg.

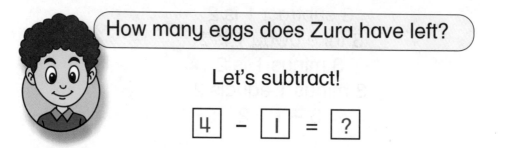

How many eggs does Zura have left?

Let's subtract!

4 – 1 = ?

How do we subtract using the abacus?

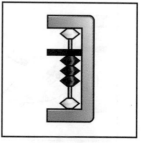

STEP 1:
up 4

STEP 2:
down 1

STEP 3:
equals 3

4 minus 1 equals 3
4 – 1 = 3

Zura has 3 eggs left!

Ah Wai has 4 balloons. 2 balloons burst!

How many balloons are left?

Let's subtract!

4 – 2 = ?

How do we subtract using the abacus?

STEP 1:
up 4

STEP 2:
down 2

STEP 3:
equals 2

4 – 2 = 2

Ah Wai has 2 balloons left!

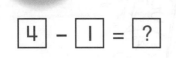 Let's practise!

$4 - 1 = ?$

STEP 1:
up 4

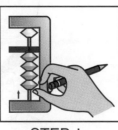

STEP 2:
down 1

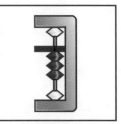

STEP 3:
equals 3

$4 - 3 = ?$

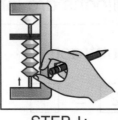

STEP 1:
up 4

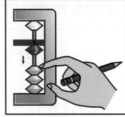

STEP 2:
down 3

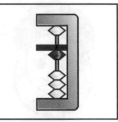

STEP 3:
equals 1

$3 - 2 = ?$

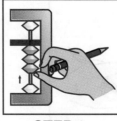

STEP 1:
up 3

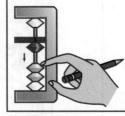

STEP 2:
down 2

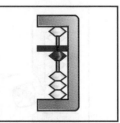

STEP 3:
equals 1

$1 - 1 = ?$

STEP 1:
up 1

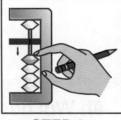

STEP 2:
down 1

STEP 3:
equals 0

There are 9 pupils
in the school bus.

3 pupils get off
the bus.

How many pupils are left in the bus?
Let's subtract!

9 – 3 = ?

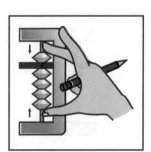

STEP 1:
up 9

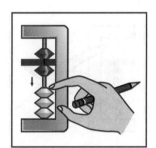

STEP 2:
down 3

STEP 3:
equals 6

9 – 3 = 6

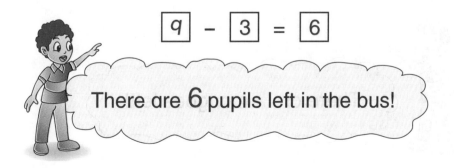

There are 6 pupils left in the bus!

There are 8 mangoes on the tree.
A monkey takes away 6 mangoes.

How many mangoes are left?
Let's subtract!

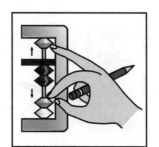

STEP 1:
up 8

STEP 2:
down 6

STEP 3:
equals 2

8 − 6 = 2

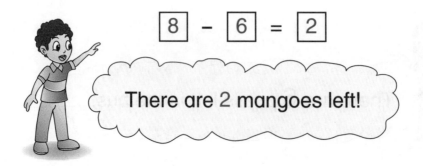

There are 2 mangoes left!

 Let's visualise!

What is $9 - 2$?

Step 1: 9, up 9

Step 2:   minus 2,
down 2

Step 3:   equals 7

$$9 - 2 = 7$$

Let's visualise!

What is 8 − 5?

Step 1: **8, up 8**

Step 2: **minus 5, down 5**

Step 3: **equals 3**

$$8 - 5 = 3$$

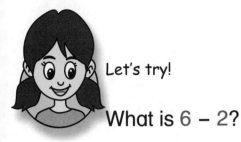 Let's try!

What is 6 − 2?

Step 1: **6, up 6**

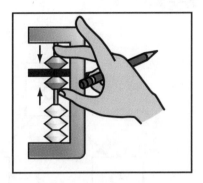

Step 2: **minus 2,
down 2?**

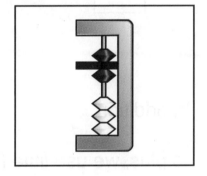

But there are not enough
lower beads!

Use little friend?

**What is the
little friend of 2?**

**How do we use
the little friend?**

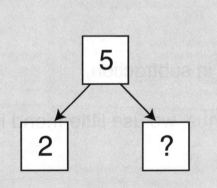

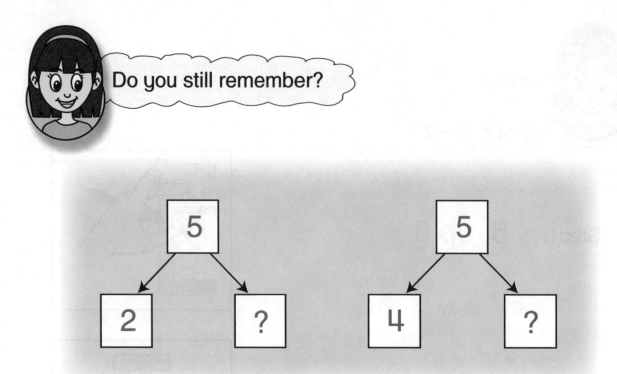

In addition,

to plus, we use little friend like this:

Up 5, Down little friend

Now, in subtraction,

to minus, we use little friend like this:

Up little friend, Down 5

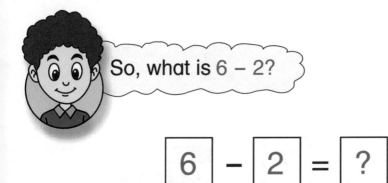

So, what is 6 – 2?

| 6 | – | 2 | = | ? |

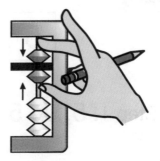

Step 1: **6, up 6**

Step 2 : **minus 2, down 2?**

But there are not enough lower beads.

USE THE LITTLE FRIEND OF 2!

Think! What is the little friend of 2?
The little friend of 2 is 3.

| 5 |
| 2 | 3 |

Up little friend, Down 5.

So, **Up 3, Down 5**

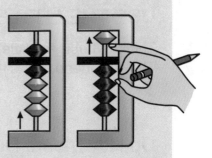

Step 3: **equals 4**

| 6 | – | 2 | = | 4 |

Let's practise!

$$5 - 1 = \ ?$$

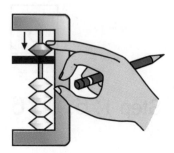

Step 1: 5, up 5

Step 2 : minus 1, down 1?

But there are not enough lower beads.

USE THE LITTLE FRIEND OF 1!

Think! What is the little friend of 1?
The little friend of 1 is 4.

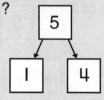

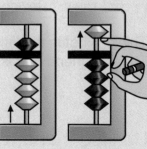

Up little friend, Down 5.

So, Up 4, Down 5

Step 3: equals 4

$$5 - 1 = 4$$

 Let's practise!

$$6 - 3 = ?$$

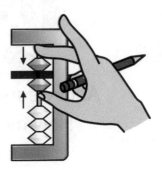

Step 1: 6, up 6

Step 2 : minus 3, down 3?

But there are not enough lower beads.

USE THE LITTLE FRIEND OF 3!

Think! What is the little friend of 3?
The little friend of 3 is 2.

5
3   2

Up little friend, Down 5.

So, Up 2, Down 5

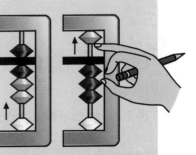

Step 3: equals 3

$$6 - 3 = 3$$

 Let's subtract!

Andi wears 7 rings.　　He removes 4 rings.

How many rings does Andi wear now?

Let's use the abacus to calculate!

$$7 - 4 = ?$$

Step 1: 7, up 7

Step 2 : minus 4, down 4?

But there are not enough lower beads.

USE LITTLE FRIEND OF 4!
The little friend of 4 is 1.

So, Up 1, Down 5

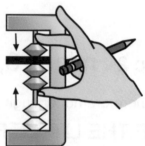

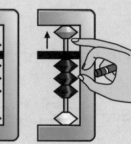

Step 3: equals 3

$$7 - 4 = 3$$

Let's subtract zero!

There are 3 fish in the bowl.

The cat does not grab any fish.

How many fish is still left in the bowl?

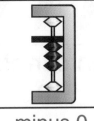

up 3   minus 0   equals 3

$$3 - 0 = 3$$

Let's try the following!

5 - 0 = ?

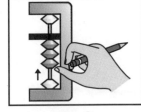

up 5   minus 0   equals 5

10 - 0 = ?

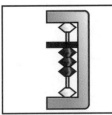

up 10   minus 0   equals 10

Subtracting zero from a number equals the number itself!

Unit 5 Numbers up to 20

Let's say!

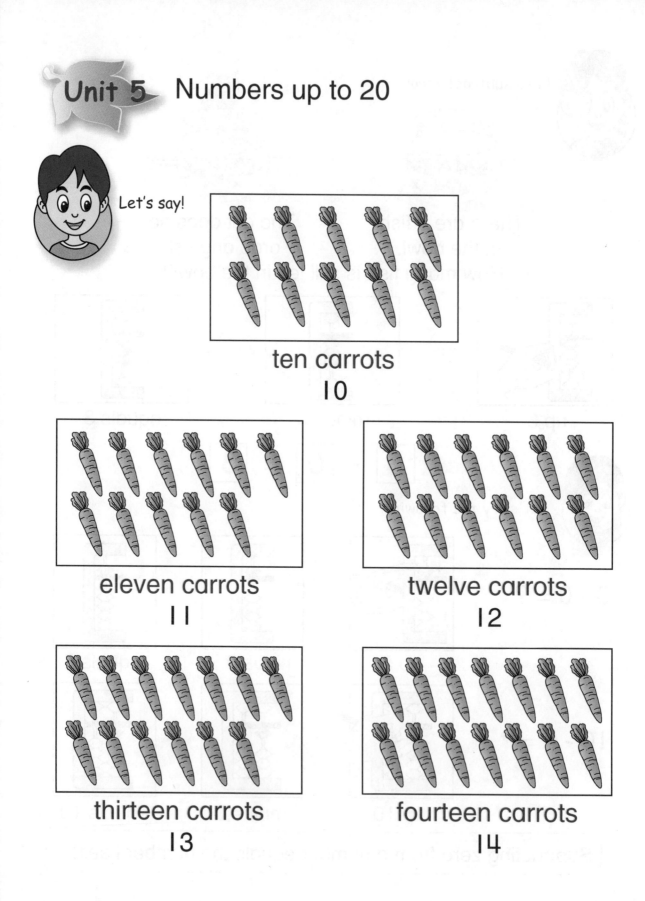

ten carrots
10

eleven carrots
11

twelve carrots
12

thirteen carrots
13

fourteen carrots
14

fifteen carrots
15

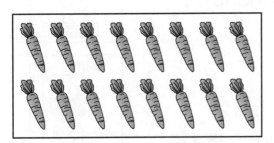

sixteen carrots
16

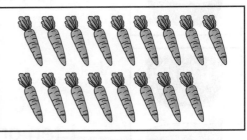

seventeen carrots
17

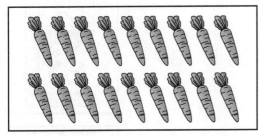

eighteen carrots
18

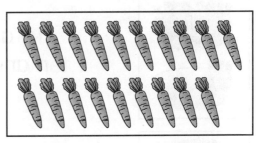

nineteen carrots
19

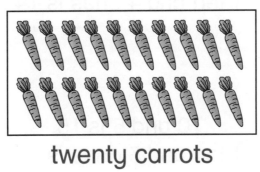

twenty carrots
20

10 and 1 is 11
1 ten and 1 one is 11

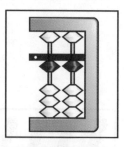

10 and 2 is 12
1 ten and 2 ones is 12

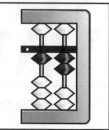

10 and 3 is 13
1 ten and 3 ones is 13

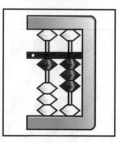

10 and 4 is 14
1 ten and 4 ones is 14

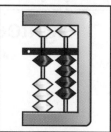

10 and 5 is 15
1 ten and 5 ones is 15

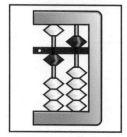

 Let's read aloud!

 10 and 6 is 16
I ten **and** 6 ones **is** 16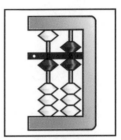

 10 and 7 is 17
I ten **and** 7 ones **is** 17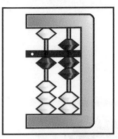

 10 and 8 is 18
I ten **and** 8 ones **is** 18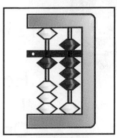

10 and 9 is 19
I ten **and** 9 ones **is** 19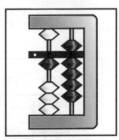

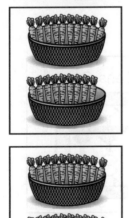 10 **and** 10 is 20
I ten **and** 10 ones **is** 20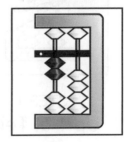

Place Value on the Abacus

One lower bead at Ones represents 1.
One lower bead at Tens represents 10.

Let's try!

How do you move up 11?
11 is 1 ten and 1 one.
One lower bead at Tens represents 10.
1 lower bead at Ones represents 1.

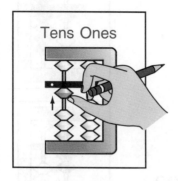

STEP 1
Up 1 at Tens

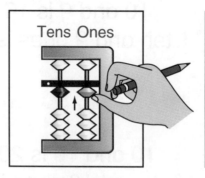

STEP 2
Up 1 at Ones

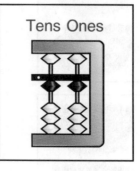

11

Let's practise!

12
twelve

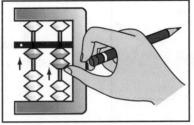

up 12
(up 1 at Tens,
up 2 at Ones)

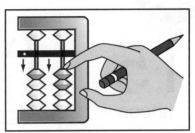

down 12
(down 1 at Tens,
down 2 at Ones)

13
thirteen

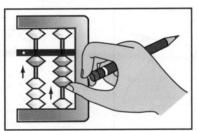

up 13
(up 1 at Tens,
up 3 at Ones)

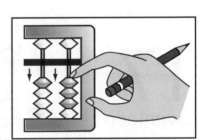

down 13
(down 1 at Tens,
down 3 at Ones)

14
fourteen

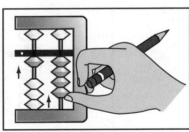

up 14
(up 1 at Tens,
up 4 at Ones)

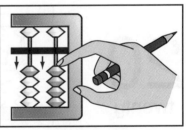

down 14
(down 1 at Tens,
down 4 at Ones)

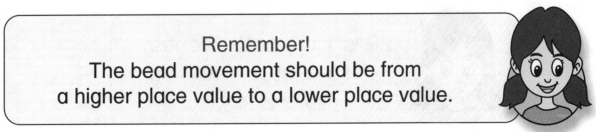

Remember!
The bead movement should be from
a higher place value to a lower place value.

 Let's practise!

15
fifteen

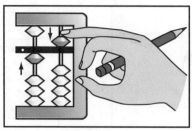

up 15
(up 1 at Tens,
up 5 at Ones)

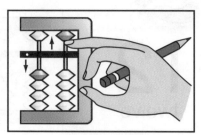

down 15
(down 1 at Tens,
down 5 at Ones)

17
seventeen

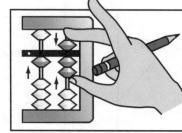

up 17
(up 1 at Tens,
up 7 at Ones)

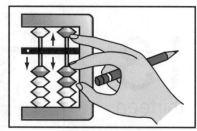

down 17
(down 1 at Tens,
down 7 at Ones)

20
twenty

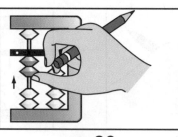

up 20
(up 2 at Tens)

down 20
(down 2 at Tens)

 20 is 1 ten and 10 ones.
10 ones is 1 ten.
20 is 2 tens.

 Let's write and visualise!

| **11** | I I | |

__eleven__

| **12** | I 2 | |

__twelve__

| **13** | I 3 | |

__thirteen__

| **14** | I 4 | |

__fourteen__

 Let's write and visualise!

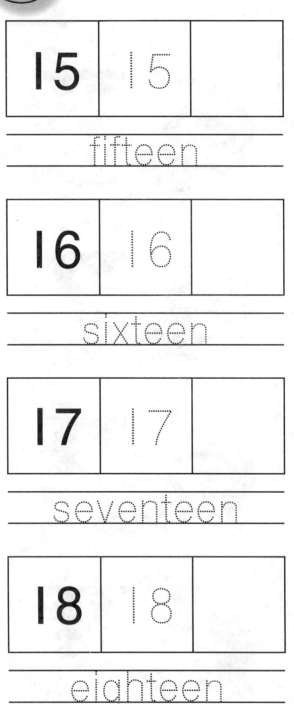

15 | 5 | |
fifteen

16 | 6 | |
sixteen

17 | 7 | |
seventeen

18 | 8 | |
eighteen

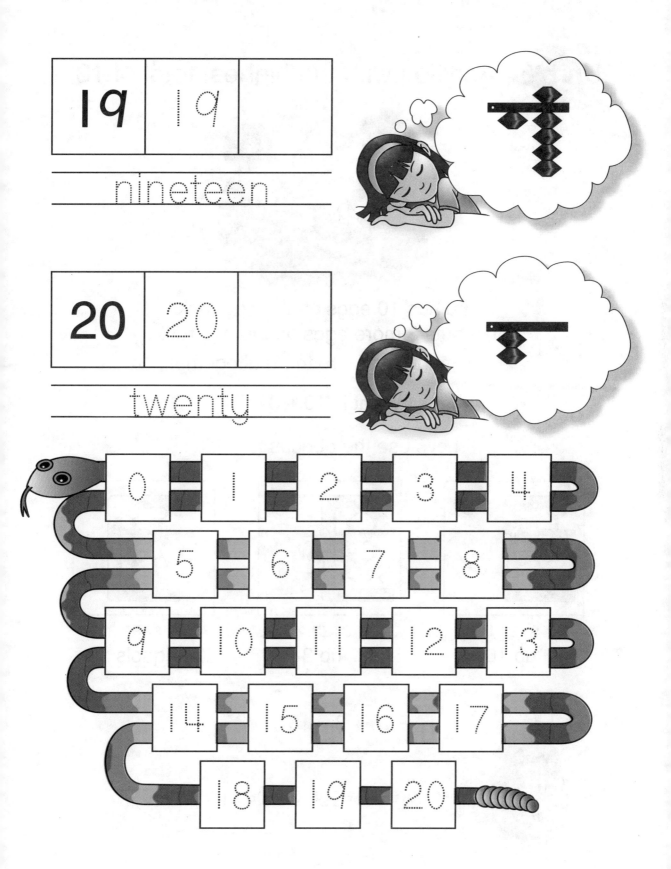

19 | 19 |
nineteen

20 | 20 |
twenty

0 1 2 3 4
5 6 7 8
9 10 11 12 13
14 15 16 17
18 19 20

Unit 6 Addition with the highest total of 18

Zura has 10 eggs on the egg rack.
Andi puts 3 more eggs on the egg rack.

How many eggs are there altogether?

What is 10 + 3?

Let's use the abacus to add!

STEP 1:
up 10

STEP 2:
up 3

STEP 3:
equals 13

$$10 + 3 = 13$$

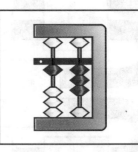

There are 13 eggs on the egg rack!

Ah Wai has 11 marbles.

Andi has 6 marbles more than Ah Wai.

How many marbles does Andi have?

Andi has 11 and 6 more marbles.

Let's add 11 and 6!

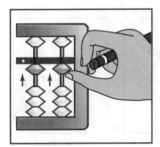

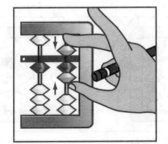

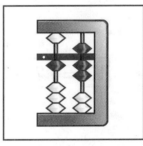

STEP 1:
up 11

STEP 2:
up 6

STEP 3:
equals 17

11 + 6 = 17

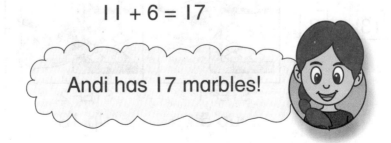

Andi has 17 marbles!

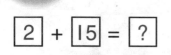 $2 + 15 = ?$

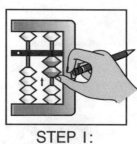 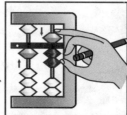 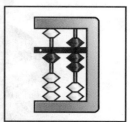

STEP 1:
up 2

STEP 2:
up 15

STEP 3:
equals 17

$11 + 3 = ?$

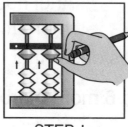 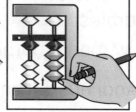 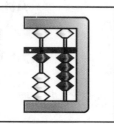

STEP 1:
up 11

STEP 2:
up 3

STEP 3:
equals 14

$7 + 10 = ?$

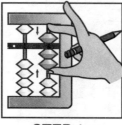 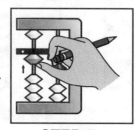 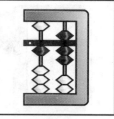

STEP 1:
up 7

STEP 2:
up 10

STEP 3:
equals 17

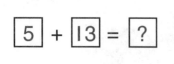 $5 + 13 = ?$

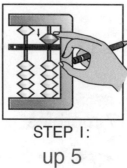 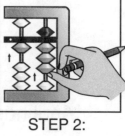 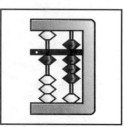

STEP 1:
up 5

STEP 2:
up 13

STEP 3:
equals 18

 Let's visualise!

What is 2 + 11?

Step 1:   **2, up 2**

Step 2:   **plus 11, up 11**

Step 3:   **equals 13**

$$2 + 11 = 13$$

Let's count the fruits!

How many red apples? 1
How many green apples? 9
How many apples altogether?
There are 10 apples altogether.

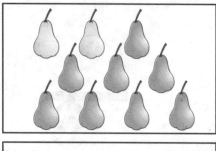

How many yellow pears? 2
How many green pears? 8
How many pears altogether?
There are 10 pears altogether.

How many green bananas? 3
How many yellow bananas? 7
How many bananas altogether?
There are 10 bananas altogether.

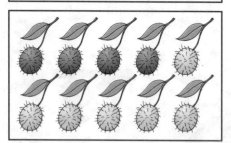

How many red rambutans? 4
How many yellow rambutans? 6
How many rambutans altogether?
There are 10 rambutans altogether.

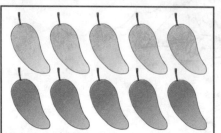

How many yellow mangoes? 5
How many green mangoes? 5
How many mangoes altogether?
There are 10 mangoes altogether.

The Big Friend!

The big friend of 1 is 9
The big friend of 9 is 1

The big friend of 2 is 8
The big friend of 8 is 2

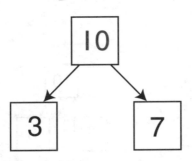

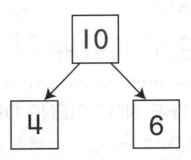

The big friend of 3 is 7
The big friend of 7 is 3

The big friend of 4 is 6
The big friend of 6 is 4

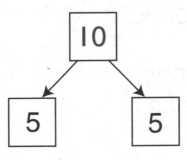

The big friend of 5 is 5

How do we use the big friend to add?
Down big friend at Ones,
Carry 1 at Tens.

Let's try!

$$8 + 2 = ?$$

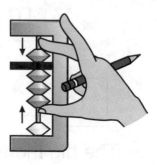

Step 1: 8, up 8

Step 2 : plus 2, up 2?

But there are not enough beads at Ones.

USE THE BIG FRIEND OF 2!

Think! What is the big friend of 2?
The big friend of 2 is 8.

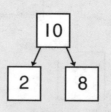

Down big friend at Ones,
Carry 1 at Tens.

So, Down 8 at Ones,
Carry 1 at Tens.

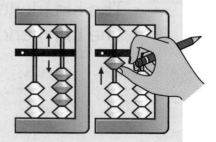

Step 3: equals 10

$$8 + 2 = 10$$

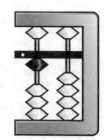

Let's try!

$$7 + 4 = ?$$

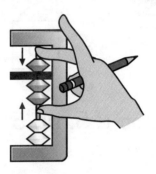

Step 1: 7, up 7

Step 2 : plus 4, up 4?

But there are not enough beads at Ones.

USE THE BIG FRIEND OF 4!

Think! What is the big friend of 4?
The big friend of 4 is 6.

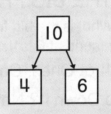

Down big friend at Ones,
Carry 1 at Tens.

So, Down 6 at Ones,
Carry 1 at Tens.

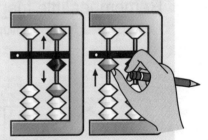

Step 3: equals 11

$$7 + 4 = 11$$

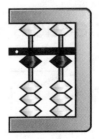

Let's try!

$$5 + 6 = ?$$

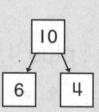

Step 1: 5, up 5

Step 2 : plus 6, up 6?

But there are not enough beads at Ones.

USE THE BIG FRIEND OF 6!

Think! What is the big friend of 6?
The big friend of 6 is 4.

Down 4 at Ones, Carry 1 at Tens.

How to Down 4? Not enough beads!
Remember little friend of 4?
Down 4→Up 1, Down 5

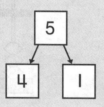

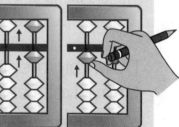

So, Up 1, Down 5, Carry 1 at Tens.

Step 3: equals 11

$$5 + 6 = 11$$

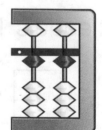

Let's try!

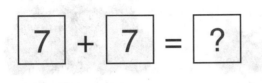

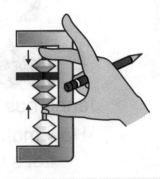

Step 1: 7, up 7

Step 2 : plus 7, up 7?

But there are not enough beads at Ones.

USE THE BIG FRIEND OF 7!

Think! What is the big friend of 7?
The big friend of 7 is 3.

Down 3 at Ones, Carry 1 at Tens.

How to Down 3? Not enough beads!
Remember little friend of 3?
Down 3→Up 2, Down 5

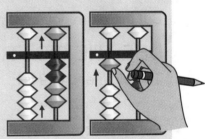

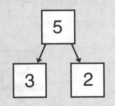

So, **Up 2, Down 5, Carry 1 at Tens.**

Step 3: equals 14

$$7 + 7 = 14$$

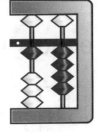

Let's add!

Jenny has 5 durians.   Andi has 9 durians.

How many durians are there altogether?
Let's use the abacus to calculate!

$$5 + 9 = ?$$

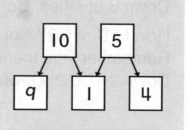

Step 1: 5, up 5

Step 2 : plus 9, up 9?

But there are not enough beads at Ones.

USE THE BIG FRIEND OF 9!

The big friend of 9 is 1.

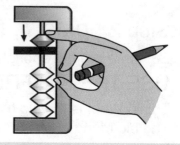

So, Down 1 at Ones, Carry 1 at Tens.
Not enough beads to Down 1.
So, Up 4, Down 5 at Ones,
        Carry 1 at Tens.

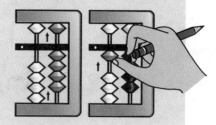

Step 3: equals 14

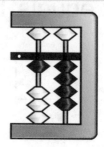

$$5 + 9 = 14$$

Let's add!

Devi has 8 roses.
Jenny has 6 more roses than Devi.
How many roses does Jenny have?

$$\boxed{8} + \boxed{6} = \boxed{?}$$

Step 1: **8, up 8**

Step 2 : **plus 6, up 6?**

But there are not enough beads at Ones.

USE THE BIG FRIEND OF 6!

The big friend of 6 is 4.

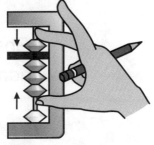

So, Down 4 at Ones, Carry 1 at Tens.
Not enough beads to Down 4.

So, Up 1, Down 5 at Ones,
        Carry 1 at Tens.

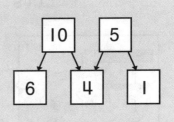

Step 3: **equals 14**

$$\boxed{8} + \boxed{6} = \boxed{14}$$

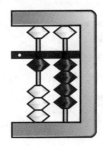

 # Unit 7 — Subtraction within the range of 18

Zura has 15 oranges.
She gives 5 oranges to Andi.
How many oranges does Zura have left?

What is 15 – 5?

Let's use the abacus to subtract!

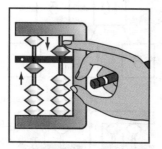

STEP 1:
up 15

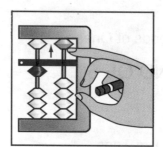

STEP 2:
down 5

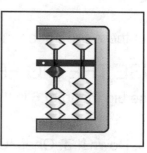

STEP 3:
equals 10

$$15 - 5 = 10$$

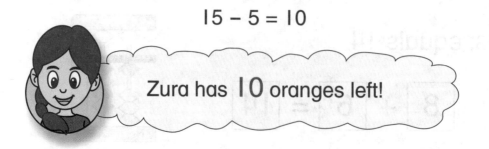

Zura has 10 oranges left!

Ah Wai has 18 marbles.

Andi has 6 marbles less than Ah Wai.

How many marbles does Andi have?

Andi has 6 less marbles than 18.

Let's subtract 6 from 18.

What is 18 − 6?

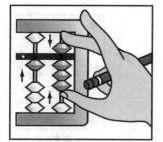

STEP 1:
up 18

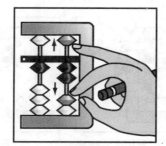

STEP 2:
down 6

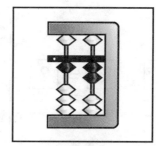

STEP 3:
equals 12

$$18 - 6 = 12$$

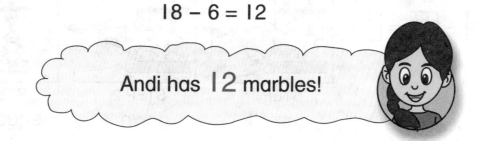

Andi has 12 marbles!

Let's practise!

$11 - 1 = ?$

 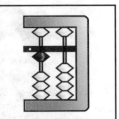

STEP 1:	STEP 2:	STEP 3:
up 11	down 1	equals 10

$16 - 10 = ?$

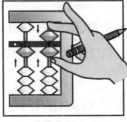  

STEP 1:	STEP 2:	STEP 3:
up 16	down 10	equals 6

$17 - 5 = ?$

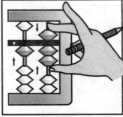 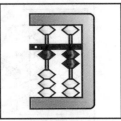

STEP 1:	STEP 2:	STEP 3:
up 17	down 5	equals 12

$14 - 3 = ?$

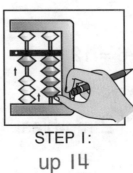 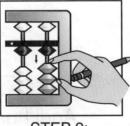 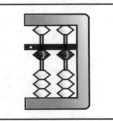

STEP 1:	STEP 2:	STEP 3:
up 14	down 3	equals 11

 Let's visualise!

What is 18 – 5?

Step 1:   18, up 18

Step 2:   minus 5,
down 5

Step 3:   equals 13

18 – 5 = 13

Remember the Big Friend?

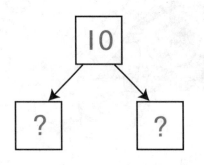

The **big friend of** 1 **is** 9
The **big friend of** 2 **is** 8
The **big friend of** 3 **is** 7
The **big friend of** 4 **is** 6
The **big friend of** 5 **is** 5
The **big friend of** 6 **is** 4
The **big friend of** 7 **is** 3
The **big friend of** 8 **is** 2
The **big friend of** 9 **is** 1

Remember!

To add, Down Big Friend at Ones, Carry 1 at Tens.

How do we use the big friend to subtract?

To subtract, Remove 1 at Tens, Up Big Friend at Ones.

 Let's try!

$$\boxed{15} - \boxed{9} = \boxed{?}$$

Step 1: 15, up 15

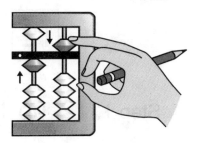

Step 2 : minus 9, down 9?

But there are not enough beads at Ones.

USE THE BIG FRIEND OF 9!

Think! What is the big friend of 9?
The big friend of 9 is 1.

Remove 1 at Tens.
Up Big Friend at Ones.

So, Remove 1 at Tens,
Up 1 at Ones.

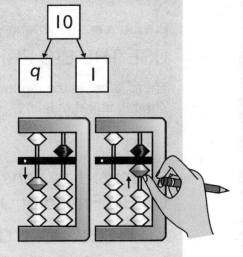

Step 3: equals 6

$$\boxed{15} - \boxed{9} = \boxed{6}$$

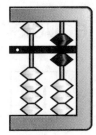

 Let's try!

$$\boxed{12} - \boxed{8} = \boxed{?}$$

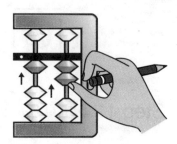

Step 1: 12, up 12

Step 2 : minus 8, down 8?

But there are not enough beads at Ones.

USE THE BIG FRIEND OF 8!

Think! What is the big friend of 8?
The big friend of 8 is 2.

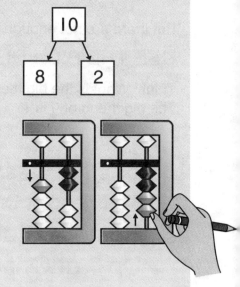

Remove 1 at Tens.
Up Big Friend at Ones.

So, Remove 1 at Tens,
    Up 2 at Ones.

Step 3: equals 4

$$\boxed{12} - \boxed{8} = \boxed{4}$$

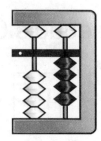

Let's try!

$$11 - 6 = ?$$

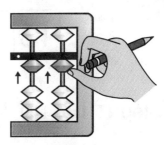

Step 1: 11, up 11

Step 2 : minus 6, down 6?

But there are not enough beads at Ones.

USE THE BIG FRIEND OF 6!

Think! What is the big friend of 6?
The big friend of 6 is 4.

Remove 1 at Tens, Up 4 at Ones.

How to Up 4? Not enough beads!
Remember little friend of 4?
Up 4→Up 5, Down 1

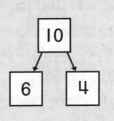

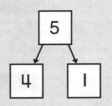

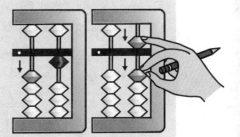

So, Remove 1 at Tens,
     Up 5, Down 1 at Ones.

Step 3: equals 5

$$11 - 6 = 5$$

 Let's try!

$$13 - 7 = ?$$

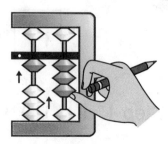

Step 1: 13, up 13

Step 2 : minus 7, down 7?

But there are not enough beads at Ones.

USE THE BIG FRIEND OF 7!

Think! What is the big friend of 7?
The big friend of 7 is 3.

Remove 1 at Tens, Up 3 at Ones.

How to Up 3? Not enough beads!
Remember little friend of 3?
Up 3→Up 5, Down 2

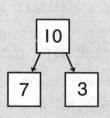

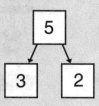

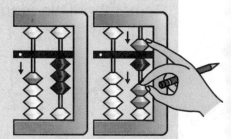

So, Remove 1 at Tens,
Up 5, Down 2 at Ones.

Step 3: equals 6

$$13 - 7 = 6$$

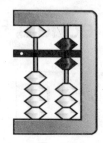

Let's subtract!

There are 14 leaves. 6 leaves fall.
How many leaves are left on the tree?
Let's use the abacus to calculate!

$$14 - 6 = \boxed{?}$$

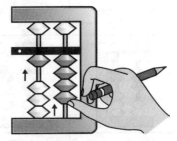

Step 1: 14, up 14

Step 2 : minus 6, down 6?

But there are not enough beads at Ones.

USE BIG FRIEND OF 6!

The big friend of 6 is 4.

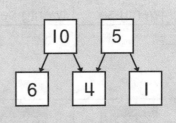

So, Remove 1 at Tens, Up 4 at Ones.
Not enough beads to Up 4.
So, Remove 1 at Tens,
    Up 5, Down 1 at Ones.

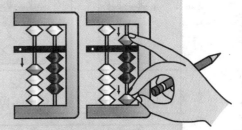

Step 3: equals 8

$$14 - 6 = \boxed{8}$$

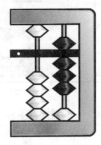

Unit 8 Numbers up to 100

Let's look at the beads and say out loud!

21 twenty-one	22 twenty-two	23 twenty-three	24 twenty-four	25 twenty-five
26 twenty-six	27 twenty-seven	28 twenty-eight	29 twenty-nine	30 thirty

31 thirty-one	32 thirty-two	33 thirty-three	34 thirty-four	35 thirty-five
36 thirty-six	37 thirty-seven	38 thirty-eight	39 thirty-nine	40 forty

41 forty-one	42 forty-two	43 forty-three	44 forty-four	45 forty-five
46 forty-six	47 forty-seven	48 forty-eight	49 forty-nine	50 fifty

51 fifty-one	52 fifty-two	53 fifty-three	54 fifty-four	55 fifty-five
56 fifty-six	57 fifty-seven	58 fifty-eight	59 fifty-nine	60 sixty

61 sixty-one	62 sixty-two	63 sixty-three	64 sixty-four	65 sixty-five
66 sixty-six	67 sixty-seven	68 sixty-eight	69 sixty-nine	70 seventy

71 seventy-one	72 seventy-two	73 seventy-three	74 seventy-four	75 seventy-five
76 seventy-six	77 seventy-seven	78 seventy-eight	79 seventy-nine	80 eighty

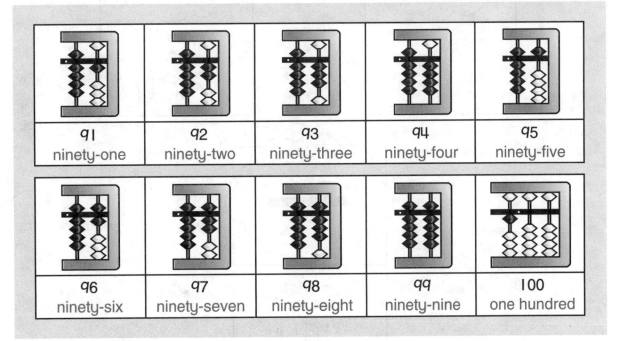

| 81 eighty-one | 82 eighty-two | 83 eighty-three | 84 eighty-four | 85 eighty-five |
| 86 eighty-six | 87 eighty-seven | 88 eighty-eight | 89 eighty-nine | 90 ninety |

| 91 ninety-one | 92 ninety-two | 93 ninety-three | 94 ninety-four | 95 ninety-five |
| 96 ninety-six | 97 ninety-seven | 98 ninety-eight | 99 ninety-nine | 100 one hundred |

Let's write and read!

10
ten

20
twenty

30
thirty

40
forty

50
fifty

60
sixty

70
seventy

80
eighty

90
ninety

100
one hundred

Notes